# Jumpers

Cynthia Rider

OXFORD
UNIVERSITY PRESS

Dogs are good jumpers.

They jump for balls and sticks.

Dolphins jump for fun.

They jump out of the water.

Penguins jump out of the water.

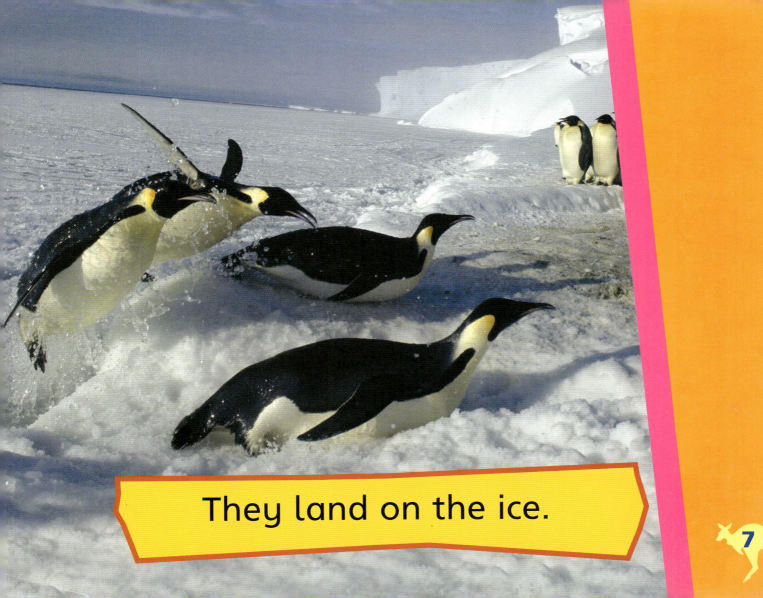

They land on the ice.

Squirrels can jump from tree to tree.

Their bushy tails help them to balance.

Whales have big strong tails.

Their tails help them to jump out of the water.

Kangaroos are very good jumpers.

They jump along on their strong back legs.

Frogs have long back legs.

Their long legs help them to jump out of the water.